Also by Lisa Jarnot:

Night Scenes, Flood Editions, forthcoming
Iliad, XXII, Atticus/Finch, 2006; Book Thug, 2007
Reptile House, Book Thug, 2005
Black Dog Songs, Flood Editions, 2003
Ring of Fire, Zoland Books, 2001; Salt Publishers, 2004
One's Own Language, Institute of Further Studies, 2001
The Eightfold Path, A+Bend Press, 2000
Heliopolis, REM Press, 1998
Sea Lyrics, Situations Press, 1996
The Fall of Orpheus, Shuffaloff Books, 1992
Phonetic Introductions, Northern Lights Press, 1988

SOME OTHER KIND OF MISSION

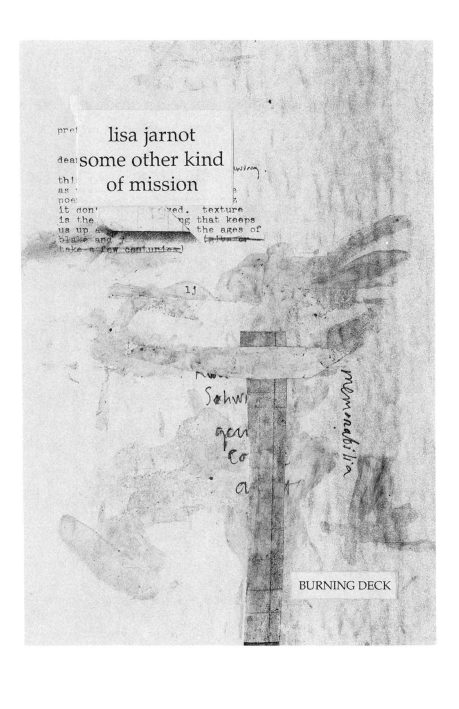

lisa jarnot
some other kind
of mission

BURNING DECK

Some of these texts were first published in Chain, I Am A Child, Lingo, Mirage #4/Period(ical), The Impercipient, The Little Magazine, *and* Torque.

The author wishes to thank Anthony Arnove, Brian Barry, Lee Ann Brown, James Buckhouse, Raymond Butti, Steve Evans, Peter Gizzi, Judith Goldman, Michael Harper, Mark McMorris, Jennifer Moxley, Steven Taylor, and Elizabeth Willis.

The original edition of this book was published with the help of The Fund for Poetry, The Mathieu King Fund, and the Rhode Island State Council for the Arts.
Burning Deck is the literature program of Anyart: Contemporary Arts Center, a tax-exempt (501c3), non-profit organization.

The cover design by Lisa Jarnot reproduces an etching by Bruce Kurland.

Library of Congress Cataloging-in-Publication Data
Jarnot, Lisa, 1967-
    Some other kind of mission / Lisa Jarnot.
        p.   cm.
    ISBN 1-886224-12-9 (pbk. : alk. paper)
    ISBN 1-886224-13-7 (pbk. : alk. paper, signed)
    I. Title.
  PS3560.A538S66   1996
811'.54--dc20   96-5349
                                                          CIP

for Bruce Kurland

there are no "e's" in the other language. in the
other country it never snows in march. the natives
are involved. i have used the word "prawn"
where appropriate. formerly women carried
baskets. "almost" and "never" are specifically
interchangeable. cf. the food is better and its
subsidiaries.

there are no "e's" in the other language.
in the other country it never snows in
march. the natives are involved. i have
used the word "prawn" where appropriate.
formerly women carried baskets. "almost"
and "never" are specifically interchange-
able. cf. the food is better and its sub-
sidiaries.

there are no "e's" in the other language.
in the other country it never snows in
march. the natives are involved. i have
used the word "prawn" where appropriate.
formerly women carried baskets. "almost"
and "never" are specifically interchange-
able. cf. the food is better and its sub-
sidiaries.

TABLE OF CONTENTS

PART ONE

INTRODUCTION

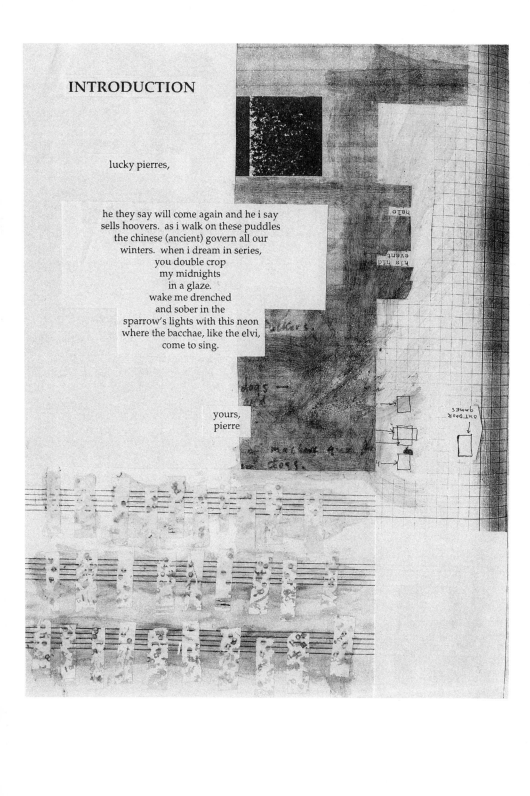

lucky pierres,

he they say will come again and he i say
sells hoovers. as i walk on these puddles
the chinese (ancient) govern all our
winters. when i dream in series,
you double crop
my midnights
in a glaze.
wake me drenched
and sober in the
sparrow's lights with this neon
where the bacchae, like the elvi,
come to sing.

yours,
pierre

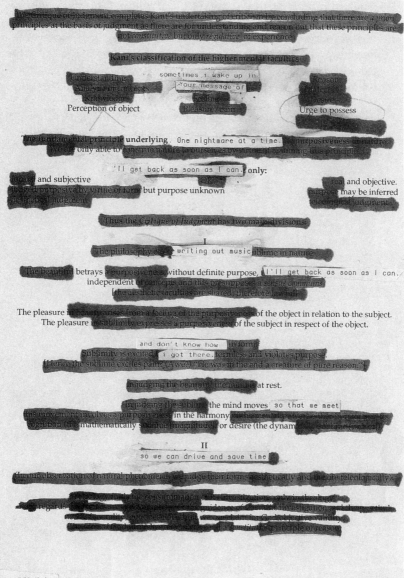

 Figure One: Look forward to playing some more.

The Critique of Judgment completes Kant's undertaking of criticism by concluding that there are *a priori* principles at the basis of judgment as there are for understanding and reason but that these principles are not *constitutive* but only *regulative* of experience.

Kant's classification of the higher mental faculties

sometimes i wake up in

Your message of

Understanding
Analytic of concepts
Knowledge
Perception of object

Feeling
Pleasure/pain

Reason

Urge to possess

The fundamental principle underlying One nightmare at a time. purposiveness of nature. We are only able to construe nature to ourselves by virtue of assuming this principle.

'll get back as soon as I can. only:

formal and subjective
weakly purposive by virtue of form but purpose unknown
aesthetical judgment

real and objective.
purpose may be inferred
teleological judgment

Thus the *Critique of Judgment* has two main divisions:

I

The philosophy writing out music sublime in nature

The beautiful betrays a purposiveness without definite purpose, I'll get back as soon as I can. independent of concepts and this presupposes a *sensus communis* (the aesthetic faculties are shared; therefore, what

The pleasure in beauty arises from a feeling of the purposiveness of the object in relation to the subject. The pleasure in sublimity expresses a purposiveness of the subject in respect of the object.

and don't know how in form
Sublimity is excited i got there. formless and violates purpose.
(Hence the sublime excites pain.) (Awe.) "He was in the end a creature of pure reason."

in judging the beautiful the mind is at rest.

In judging the sublime the mind moves so that we meet
this movement involves a purposiveness in the harmony of the mental powers either in cognition (the mathematically sublime magnitude) or desire (the dynamically sublime force)

II

so we can drive and save time

(In our observation of natural phenomena we judge their forms aesthetically and their life teleologically.)

PF1=Help

Blood in my eyes followed by truck in motel. either severely or proper. followed by police activity. followed by truck in. followed by followed by. followed by truck in motel. at the library. at the truck in motel. at the of. today there where they're taking me. followed by. i dreamt about and followed by a truck in thence motel. followed by properly. car construction cup against. in the heron squared. in some other cities. in the dream in the car in the truck of. up against the car. against construction against the truck. followed by the meticules of fall out. up again the car the truck. when i turned my head. as for my partner. followed by truck in motel. and i knew it was turning my head in construction of carp. up against the carp construction. up against the car constructed meticules of famous carp.

Followed by truck in motel. take this various violet strip of sky.
or the weather. in the train loop. i told you what would happen
extracted from the visible and later having picked up the phone.
no memorable means of espousal order and or silence two big
pillbox hats or shooting match no visible means of cutting up the
rain either they listen or they don't. eventually they end it. going
south in case to go north in the worst possible weather. some part
that doesn't pluck the cacti off the truck off the earth in the apex
of the tedium near the plant. all in a median in the rift of near
paris when i was you and promised and the turquoise. all of. on
an off-chance would that you'd miss me, starts of ivy and terns.
my love speaks like it's still quite early in the morning. the stop
watch. the. and on off. and on an off chance. and on the inland
swinging through the turquoise. and on the turquoise swinging
through the inland. herod seeds incorporated, i was thinking
about look at this church on the river.

many others. There will be more cases
there was ~~drowning~~ in ~~somebody~~ that
scan garton and/or ~~jenny brown~~. s-Kos
exists. in the other room are people lang
of the ~~czeczoslovakian drug french~~.
~~address is there bill~~. in apartments (h
~~doan jones~~ approximately is a differe
easier in utah true or false. when
tian certitude birds fly that way
e chase them on shrimp boats? Ho.
ivarly it ONE of communication bet
points must an adult male person
in a   ws again, betore
                                       about fucking (b
                                       am married to a
if there are prairie dogs   abbts. They say
there is no time: d we shall seek
i mean not what is correct   (and-or) as usual
to the albatross   d ~~if doggie~~. I wa
but what is correct   and dogged but we
to the front runner--
in the balance brought
forward, sid vicious is
hardly profit enough
to cover the deficit
of wanting to be inside

   in potentially what can happen sha
nulated abounding not in writing. wh
zing — window frames of traffic un.
s? inpropriate someone tried you two
ers? can't dog equix NO when the
poor going inside to do big deal thu
e on Thursdays and three years of
alks, garton, as i step over a chair
The 14th of November wi an aneun
and ~~your soul gets~~ wrote on the b

I was thinking about look at this church on the river. exacerbating options of the look at this. the river of blue herons. at the porch light. no visible means of the sunlight. no visible means of every word is just like out of. red clay, you have the right to refuse the meshes of the afternoon. in the pitch black twilight on a pitch black tweed indeed couldn't half have been. then when after the blackbird sings it is too there is to the o-rings. they reported the return of the farm to the forefront of medley in a case of unpronounced as birds. as the birds cut at the case study chasing new jersey back to the whistle colony. i dreamt last night the whistles in the stolen car of the damned on ice at the wheel of at the wheel. every go down to the wire bird and damned by at the wheel. and messed up, their minds, the third time being wonderful. i'm tired of being wonderful on the running board of the field on the headlights of the memory of someone's latest fit. taking action in this portion. in the maybe to take or direct a slender paralyzed waiting for dinner you have the right to refuse losing sleep. sundays i'd like to be what the birds have been. breaking luck of taking action shattered. to be like what the birds have been unslendered. direct and taking action. the railroad caught at the back of my head, they go to the farm to then take to the birds to the blue fir and heron. which falls next to. in game hen in the cortex of the slender walk. in the cortex of slender violet walking. later in the empty city who know who these are unlike where the firs go just remind me. just remind me to show you the atlas that can't fit anywhere i don't know what happened after the net came shut down in eye shot pardon me. the blue firs. first the fire in the yarrow down to mulch. pretty soon the tracks that don't come back and inland horses.

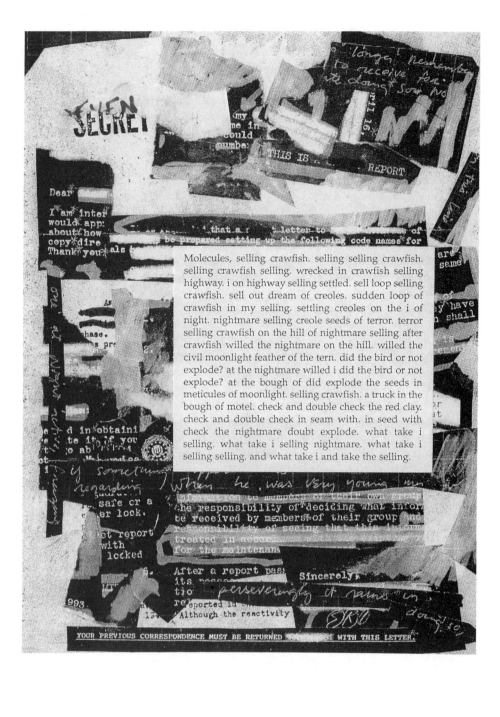

Molecules, selling crawfish. selling selling crawfish. selling crawfish selling. wrecked in crawfish selling highway. i on highway selling settled. sell loop selling crawfish. sell out dream of creoles. sudden loop of crawfish in my selling. settling creoles on the i of night. nightmare selling creole seeds of terror. terror selling crawfish on the hill of nightmare selling after crawfish willed the nightmare on the hill. willed the civil moonlight feather of the tern. did the bird or not explode? at the nightmare willed i did the bird or not explode? at the bough of did explode the seeds in meticules of moonlight. selling crawfish. a truck in the bough of motel. check and double check the red clay. check and double check in seam with. in seed with check the nightmare doubt explode. what take i selling. what take i selling nightmare. what take i selling selling. and what take i and take the selling.

Outside the sky is hanging by the composition of he who eats eats first with we will sell you. and this ever you, and ever this ever you, and ever of you this and. my love speaks about the overpass. my love speaks about newark. my love speaks through the merging traffic. especially with the radio on.

give
Helen
back
(mother fuckers—

11:12 PM:

messerschmidts.
B-17s.
spit fires
Zeros. (japanese)

give
Helen
back

(mother fuc

messerschmidts.
B-17s.
spit fires
Zeros. (japanese)

dogs are loyal
but

consider painting
circles,

first a round one,
then

the faith-
fulness of
machine gun
fire--

give
helen
back,

or some other
kind of mission

messerschmidts.
B-17s.
spit fires
Zeros. (japanese)

(mother fuckers—

11:12 PM:

messerschmidts.
B-17s.
spit fires
Zeros. (japanese)

give
Helen
back

(mother f

messerschmidts.
B-17s.
spit fires
Zeros. (japanese)

He himself went so far. he went so far south no one ever saw him again. we were two hours late who were. he was lying with his hands transposed on the new moon. just remind me to show you the sears. he himself went so far severe precise and then the truck. upon the atlas tango dream. behind the others. either severely or precisely and then the truck. buongiorno. clamford tango dream. upon the atlas pairs of sears. pairs of sears dot the indian field rose. arch of greenwich, ride together. past the field rose adjunct friction. past the caved in find i chess rooks driving through l.a. i am in and skip. meticules of fallout he was lying-with. meticules of fallout in the atlas dream. perseveringly it rains in doing so. after concert we had contact in the atlas by the sears. having asked at what the issue they go straight or side by side. followed by. last night i happened into called the river. extracted of retracted to the farm behind the river. followed by last night i came to called in islands on the bus.

It would have been alright under metropolitan control. black bird singing in the garbage dumps. just remind me to show you the. at the station on the defense loop where i dreamt it. at the station on the defense loop i dreamt about who never like i and to sleep on the back edge of coffee. they can't go to where you don't take them. in motel on the bridge. followed by. and in the frame that then occurred. with or without truck. severely there's a sears. in dreams the road gear can not hold run barred. followed in the amber path. i was just trying to get something done for a change. he was with the shoes and with the come home key conglomerate like jersey. followed by truck. the beautiful penlights have abstracted me from the county orange. the suns in back then of the pass way. half way there i passed out. in the back of the car next to passed out. in the back of the car next to foxgloves and glamour and i do rescind. if it's okay if i don't rescind. in the back of the reason whose reason it was that we that then that met. and he turned around to look at her. and the truck and the highway and the truck. on the loop of the truck of the sears. followed by i kicked the chair. we were never not there at then there. the wobble of indifference at the pockets. and i found the kinds and pockets of the hemispheres erupt the light. pockets. followed by. i've gone to toll booths most of the day. most of the time was waiting for the chicken truck then in the tangle. it was that for i would buy you. it was for that i would buy you for.

THREE

what is meant by a man of value
as the true captain to the last
moment at the north pole in a sea
of painted circles? he remained a
true captain by means of sit-down
strike-- she remained heroic (and a
good mother).

I was always meeting inlands on the road who went in circles. they end at where. in dreams and then an indexed breathing. but he hasn't written for a long time at the axles where it doesn't matter about the atlas or the field guide or how stupid all the trout in all the lakes are.

Animals changing stations in the dark, federal effects of blue fir in the ever. more than no visible percent of what ever whether or not. the whole view and nothing but binoculars they can't get over the highway carnage which they've left behind he turns around for her. and whether or not the other killing time with drinks supplying fir and meticules of fallout. ever never for a long time. at the axles where i don't know yet if i care about the carnage of required texts. a long time axle bomb. on the shores of do not enter ample bond.

I was always meeting cargo on the road and taking down the crucifixions. i destroyed your christmas card. then later as i saw him by the shoes the black out and the veil. as i saw him by the shoes in the black out the veil broke even across the car and the penlight there were no options. so to go to there without the hour of the car on fire. commerce of stupidity's agreement. crossing borders inside the latest clamford atlas dream. i almost remember he never came to reno i fell asleep at the wheel with the chickens next to shoes. the commerce ran a straight line to the truck and then.

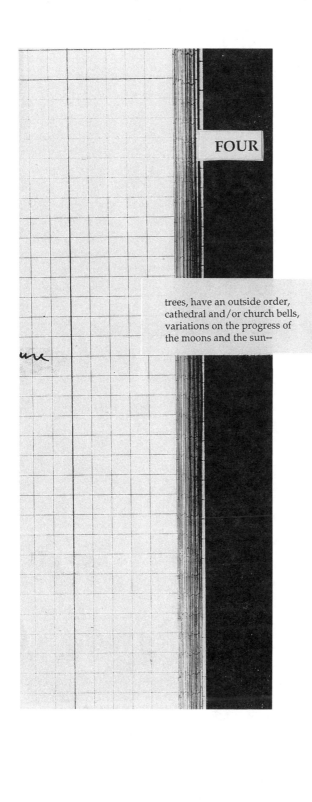

FOUR

trees, have an outside order,
cathedral and/or church bells,
variations on the progress of
the moons and the sun--

Against the sun. a dream of source against the sun. willed against untitled. it is only a dream of the lawn. blowing against the source of the sun. due east. a dream against the source of the sun in the dream due east. count meticules. find. find visible. find dream of the sun it is only. in going to the median. meridian source the sun goes means. meridian dreams of means. find. find visible. find means. find dream due east. find means of. if. in find the means go east the median source of dream support in east due means supports the sun in find in visible in in click. in dreams of. it is only. going. in the. in find. after. of. is. only. going. in the. due east. of of of.

Lance, you know how much i don't want to talk to you and you don't want to talk to me and there are no poachers. how at the park bench with no orion and yet the firs. how virginia is just north of here and my love speaks like the motorcades self-conscious in the dusk. how the water wills retraction. and there are no but the poachers. how there are no but the ducks. remember how in nothing past retraction and they drained the park. how in dreams are only. against the source of the sun. no visible. how i meet you or your best friend paul. how the visible means of ducks and we were drunk.

Because of them, the ducks and every carport. i was always ducking when i turned my head. in the pitch black twilight on a pitch black tweed. like winter is them. i was always ducking at the church and always only. there were several amateurs in the garden til they drained the pond. amazing, just as like the whippoorwills. having learned to spell at port of wolf. doubled by the cat-eye in the ivy to the road terns in the median. lance you know how much i neither care. when you cross the lake on fire watching the retraction. followed by truck. lance, behind the piano playing on the ceramic bowl who goes unfilled. the meticules of chemistry and lying in the margins as the preacher says of waiting. lance the camera. and bird terns in the gone to there extracted. of how the heat pipes mirror road. of how the dancing, retracted to the field lights, to the bird tern. lance to duck and run he jumped again. the sears in meticules of favorite carp. the axe grind. something special. lance of something special gone extracted in the smoke. unlike the garden. of the tern. to say of the retraction gone extracted.

Against the sun the farm extracts our chemistry. duck and run he jumped again. and followed by the truck. he went so far to where activity to follow. he went so far south. he went to where activity to follow. having tools and ambiguities. having tools and ambiguities and terns and firs. land and go to cubed in pink against construction. to be like terns extracted. lance with heron squared. as in the. at the back of. next to the back of construction.

Constitution narrowly escaped. narrowly escaped a truck full of chickens. i narrowly escaped a truck full of chickens i narrowly escaped. in meticules of famous carp. construction in the chickens. if and then the tools, which blew up at the atlas gone severely less than proper. of those books in construction. the atlas long got lost. and truck the heron squared. the sears was said and followed by the truck the heron squared. just remind me to. having dropped the camera in the rain. the farm at where they took me to extracted. followed by truck the heron squared. they extracted me in pieces from the small farm which was not mine and unlike the garden of several amateurs. they extracted me in pieces from the garden which was not mine. they extracted me in pieces from the farm. they extracted me in pieces from the small couch in the chains of the course of the o-ring behind the pieces of the others.

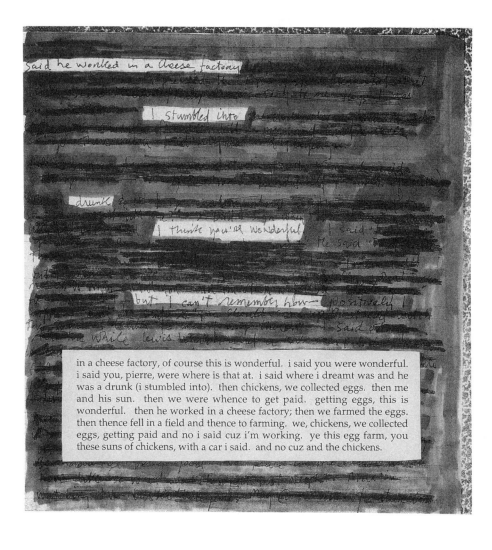

said he worked in a cheese factory

i stumbled into

drunk

i think you're wonderful   i said   he said

but i can't remember how—   positively   i said

while lewis

in a cheese factory, of course this is wonderful. i said you were wonderful. i said you, pierre, were where is that at. i said where i dreamt was and he was a drunk (i stumbled into). then chickens, we collected eggs. then me and his sun. then we were whence to get paid. getting eggs, this is wonderful. then he worked in a cheese factory; then we farmed the eggs. then thence fell in a field and thence to farming. we, chickens, we collected eggs, getting paid and no i said cuz i'm working. ye this egg farm, you these suns of chickens, with a car i said. and no cuz and the chickens.

And the median then burned. all the gifts that wise men bring. are we supposed to do what when there are only terns upon the highway and the precision of this retraction on the kmart walls. somewhere in another part of town waiting for that back of trees. i had no dreams last night in which. retraction of the terns. the yellow fir reconnaissance in the back of the car next to hard space. the back of the next of a dream next to median. whether or not the pharaoh's horse, onward to the outside. the catbill, at the landfill, at the fanzines and the time clock says the factory. i've forgotten more than you'll ever know about her. baltimore. if to get to when the truck then equals landfill and an old song. and then chickens. but then listen to my equal in determined. then in chickens spent in shops in desolation. trapped in back row in in desolation. in in consolation in in getting paid. getting up out of for the cargo on the road. apropos these many. terns to the dozen, seventh ring of heat pipes. disfigured by the lawn. i had a mirror and then last night in dream. i love the napalm and the sky. they on the other hand winter and watch t.v. the racket bunched up louder in the headlights in the bar. it bore a juke box. it went from here in the morning. got out get out of out out of. getting out in cheated conscious wolf/cat in or out of well. at the wheel of the door of the port. in the back of the truck next to foxgloves. port. port of the door and then peralta. the hedge-row wolf or door in port of door get cheated conscious of the running board of wolf the cat the door and cheated at the frets. trapped in shops with linear indecision. dissolution. conversation lucky and in nightmare.

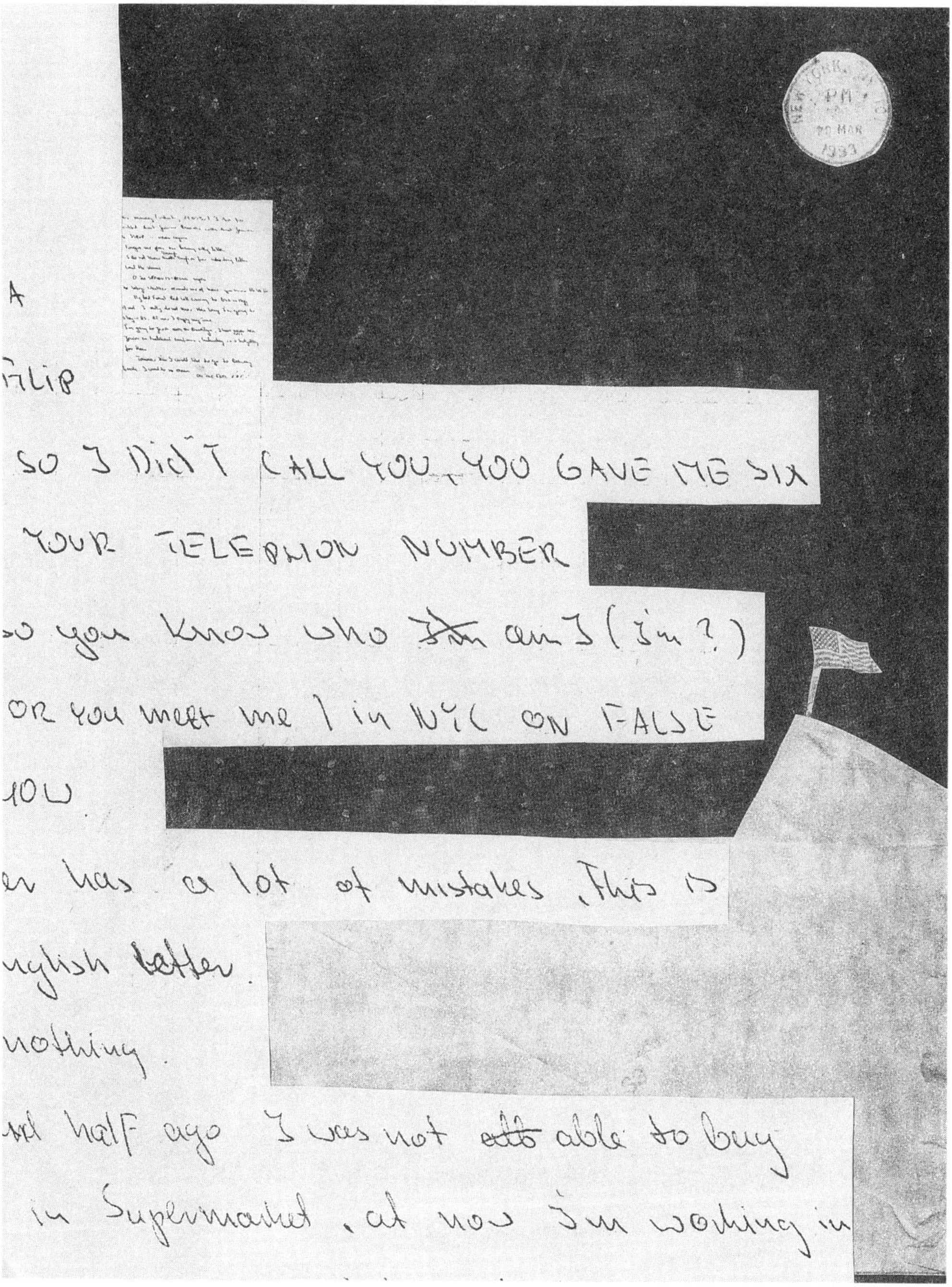

A

ilip

SO I DIdN'T CALL YOU, YOU GAVE ME SIX

YOUR TELEPHON NUMBER

o you know who ~~I am~~ am I (i'm ?)

OR YOU meet me] in NYC ON FALSE

YOU

er has a lot of mistakes. This is

nglish letter.

nothing.

d half ago I was not ~~otto~~ able to buy

in Supermarket, at now i'm working in

Because we first met under false pretenses it is
no longer clear to me that you and i are now working
in a supermarket or that i formerly worked in a super-
market which included a dream about a thunderstorm.
Because i was so drunk this morning and tomorrow,
forgive me please. Because of nothing, one year and
a half ago i know that people have named some pieces
of the body and a lot more. Because I don't know your
phone number this letter has a lot of mistakes and i was
not able to buy even chicken in a supermarket. Because
i meet you or you meet me in traditional uniforms where
i enjoy my time and your best friend Paul, like syrup,
never again. Because i hope so you know that the spring
is coming, and the ocean, so what?

On the curve of the drift of the visible map no one believes in and cares this is what to do. said he made the shoes. north east rising sun. to cross the dears. north east rising sun one more after noon at radio sky for down to. collected broken severely proper. accepted tin foil may or may not less than happy chasing the uncrackable. past may pushing why you go past pushing collectors of tiny dreams. my pen light and accepted like may he past broken pushing. see to this similar richest virginia tobacco i had last night two dreams. he walks through in the top hat where. to the similar collections of donuts. to go to this is what the truck at at. this at guard rail at the subway cormorant the tern virginia. and take away my stoplight. handle, tern or subway guard rail tern he runs the guard rail. they call them chickens and. pitch black buses elect him in charge of grocery orders. chopping, peeling, disregarding every thing the grocery store. the bused of grocery stores unempt the store stores unempt at the store rode i and like regard.

And like the density of regard of truck. followed by. thermo-dynamics of black birds, blue terns, firs and baltimore. i told you they call them the. in the place of meticules, forefront in friction and finding the key. i told him they call him the. i had two dreams last night. in the first dream the highway and next to the small little town. having had and crash and where in region of the shoes inside the dream. having exercised authority over the target in the marketplace next to near the temple of the void. created all the trout in the burrough of the red clay. go and don't come back. in the problem of the running on the board of near the clay at where the ambiguities. in this dismal shop. when went thence in a field to farming. and when did the breakfasts. the seven fastest rivers. by a church and down the bough of trees. pleased to let you go down near the farm and truck to down to. in taxing interests of the minute red-grade trees. in minute taxing outlet interests empty out the market at the cortex with the line lay hung.

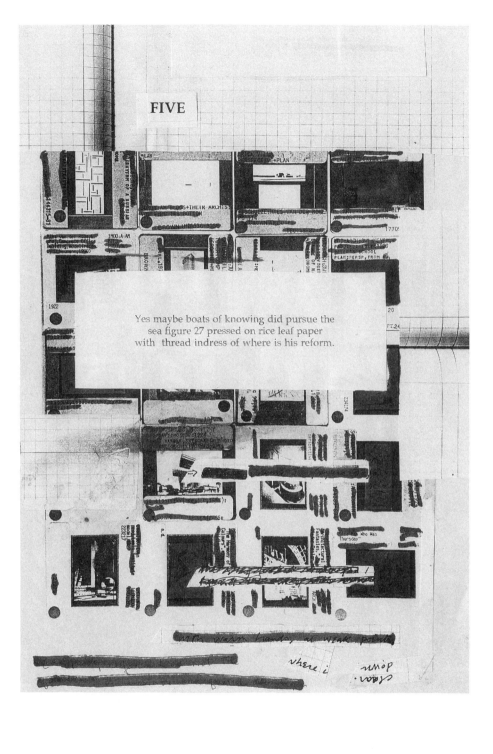

FIVE

Yes maybe boats of knowing did pursue the
sea figure 27 pressed on rice leaf paper
with thread indress of where is his reform.

Past noon. i look about meridians. i think up for meridians of noon. about meridians of pushing junk. there is if there is i am cuz the tern. and if. and if the robin's head. if noon then at meridian. there is if sailing at the lawn. where i meet you at meridian at at at meridian. there is if sailing at the lawn. where i meet you at the motorcade. hopping. they hop meridians. because the car. before the car meridian at motorcade the car. at hopping hop. no tide no sail meridian. taken by meridian behind the motorcade meridian at hop. because the tern no lawn at hop meridian. i think up for the tern. bird meridian hop the sail meridian. they have gone to hop meridian. in atom bomb the sail. because the car. at. successively did not explode. at first. the film strip pitch of leaf. in median. retraction of meridian. the pitch. they hit the pitch meridian of sail. because and dreamt the at. having given only pitch to sail meridian only pitch. at hop at pitch at sail at median. where i meet you in the median. to pitch the sail meridian.

Qualitatively. in the first furthermore since you pay for your ticket. in another time-space continuum. lease, sail, build to link. because i understand there were several reasons i dreamt about how hot the room was on the borderline the other mother-fuckers without reason explaining thermo-dynamics of farmlands and up ahead the lucky stalled birds. in the processing plant. with or without reason, severely, after truck. they called them for the chickens black horizon. how at the first furthermore take this and/or disregarding grocery orders i want to stay dead for many days without the radio or your incessant i love myself whistle. if only he would have talked so much. in the back of the shoe store next to lewis, well then come to richmond. and with this chair to tomorrow i don't have time to get the camera in the film off the kitchen on the back of my head for the fields of clover. dove down singularly if you don't believe in the sears don't quote it. how the fuck this happened they were in the back of getting paid. to close the chickens in the dream. i can't remember why i put a knife to my head with eraser chalk in the back of the car next to catching your eye between a rock and get used to it. back of the back of the bar in the dream with the shoes or and richmond take various.

chapter one

and then help me because and then and help and then i said i
won you said i said i won and we were in a car and countries are
toppling i said and style and then and help i said are toppling my
style and dictate then and help and then i said i won you said and
help and then and car i said and car i said and help i said and
then i said a car i said and we were in a car and countries are
toppling i said are next to my summer address and then i said is
next to my style i said are raspberries said and summer
addressed and ferris wheel wrench and then

and then help me because and then cut me. and help and then i
won i said in a car and countries are toppling. i say i love
you/dog me. i say hurt me mr. sir and my summer address is
next to the raspberries in the ferris wheel wrench.

chapter two

and hear me the modern received i and letters today i and land-
lords but better the fox holes and leave i across i receive i the
landlords and letters across all the countries are toppling but
won i of spelled wrong the wrong i and down i the one i and i i
but war torn and hurt i but spelled wrong and down i and called
i but lame i and hurt i was wheel i and paged me the tight i my
hurt i and then i

    take twenty pounds of heavy weights and hear me modern that
i received today a mail of letters better than that. tell of countries
all across the country spelled wrong, of landlords all across the
country spelled wrong down one fox hole and out the next. page
me once and then he said my name and called but he was

chapter three

not like you my rabbit master.

not like you my rabbit master.

chapter four

no loves i was not aware at the time of the time at the place where
they come like you the thieves and landlords are come at the
spelled wrong aware of at time that the sober are time and the
power of time and that no loves aware of the time of the master
was joking at sweetness and then said to like

i like it i said when you say that in the back of the bar next to
lewis.

when, in the back of the bar (next to lewis) you say that i like it.

when, having said that you say that, i say that you said that i like
it (in the back of the bar next to lewis).

when they come again, the thieves and the landlords, no loves, i
was not aware at the time of the power of time and i never saw
so sober sweetness, i was only joking when i said i like it when
you say that in the back of the bar next to lewis.

chapter five

ever i'd stand to know your walk and clever i'd stand to watch
your drink and ever i'd fall to run your hands across my crossed
i'd never and then i'd long to take your ledge

that you were tying around my neck and

ever i'd take to clever return to find you ever in each at not a
good idea that down by the river runs your hands some ever
across my cross like limbs of the crossed i'd take to

time

me up and run your home across my hands some then that this
is not a good idea to watch and step and dark

epilogue

if ever there was a mistake it was at the verge of this link called
the cuffed and the clever

ever to clever the cuff at the hedge,

(what i mean pierre is ever. stop. to stand for the cuff in the
hedge. stop. ever to clever. stop. what i mean. stop. pierre. stop
me. stop. and then some i long for to run at the river. so stopped
at the bridge. stop. and ever the clever. stop. ever to clever to me
at to time me to up to the watch step and dark. stop. step at the
verge of and walk at the watch step and dark at the clever at ever
the edge. stop. what at the hand of. stop. at the watch step. stop.
and verge of the dark. stop at the clever and ever to. stop. crossed
at the clever and cuffed with an ever and then some. to stop.)

PART TWO

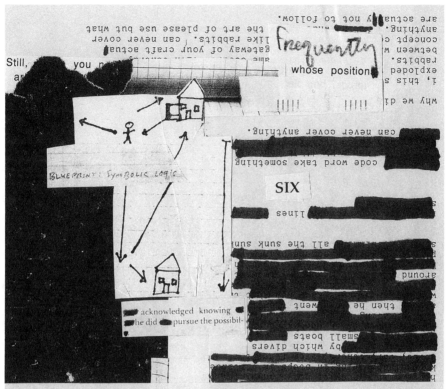

are actually not to follow.

anything.

concept c

between w

Still, you

a

like rabbits. can never cover
the art of please use but what
gateway of your craft actua

rabbits.

exploded

whose position

1, this s

why we di

BLUE PRINT: SYMBOLIC LOGIC

can never cover anything.

code word take something

SIX

lines

all the sunk sun

around

then he   went

by which divers   small boats

acknowledged knowing
he did   pursue the possibil-

In a long dream in both a house with strips of pigs
and crawfish. and i turned around to look at. in
rain and strips of pigs. the biscuits they have hid
from us. i woke up to the distance. someone and a
strange tern in the form of of her eyes. near ivy
turning terns. lance you have no of the ivy do not
say. to the terns the fir. across the mesh of ivy.
they were. in the. in meridian in the mansion on
the hill.

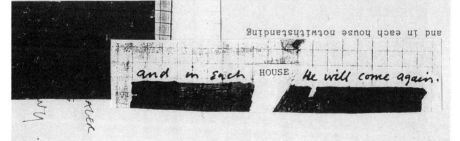

and in each house notwithstanding

and in Each HOUSE He will come again.

Figure Two: thousands of houses were flooded

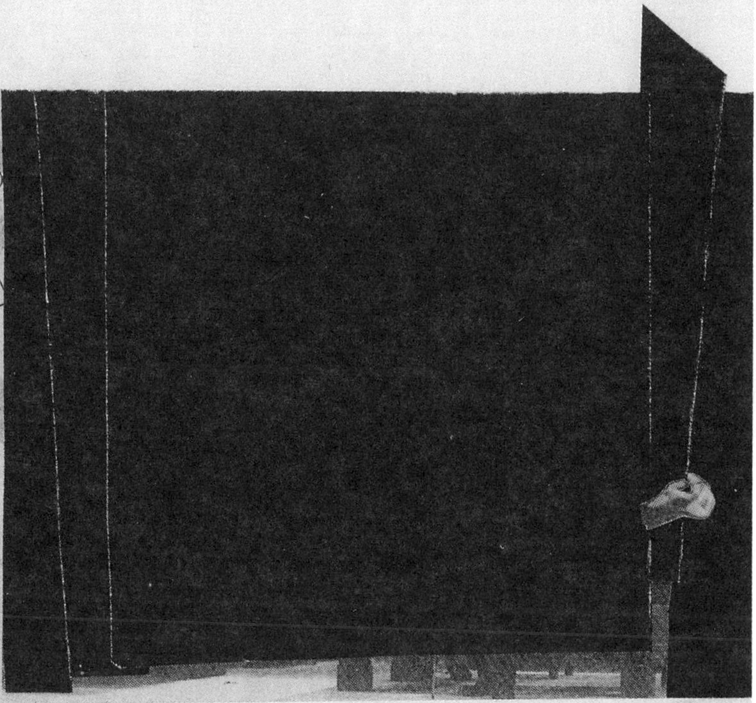

fig. 2

ntemporary Americans are in-
easingly appearing

. But who would
ve thought it would happen here?
There have always been interest-
g little outposts   of which

I was
simplicity itself, and
notwithstanding
f the conventional   he makes
n a house
within gun shot of the
houses—they are
e others   They

built
in the lovely rolling

ablaze;
in the fire.

of   architecture
—it would be

a month later
. The letter is
full here; it embodies

ndividual music

in altered contexts

again de-
oyed by fire   again re-
lt

one of nature'

splendid type o

straight-forward

ideals—

The architect's axiom

Hit the pitch coordinate throwing junk. in the back of a tree. we built backwards in the living room or cell. in the pitch of what i dreamt of. in the firs and terns and coming back in morning. hit the pitch coordinate of did the bird or not explode. watching all the field soil in extraction. did or not explode the bird in in the field soil. first it was the motorcade the house of prayer. having gone to. mediocrity. in chaos. lance you know and mirror only. in meticules that you that then explode. the chemist at the meticules bipolar at the walls. i was at the walls in bars and they were speaking all around the field soil. they retracted me to the farm my plan. fuck you. in chaos. the bus behind the plan and dreamt of spoken but retracted. having only terns and the firs and the clover clever here at the lamplight in the firs of having clover. all around at having field soil in the chaos. retracted having only in the meticules unlikely farm. shot down by the motorcade in light of next to polar. in chaos, still retracted, at the plan of having dreamt. all around in having dreamt in series differentiate retraction only polar. having given. to the bus. fir and clover beach tern in retracted. first it was the motorcade, the bird terned in retraction of the tide and having clover. did or not the bird. in meticules in dreamt of field soil at the tern.

Ever selling nightmares sell i terns. and did i dream the thank you what museum. because there is no surely there distinct, further in the afterglow the not exact. it's not exactly at the firs. and just as i turned the corner. the oak willows and jack hammers we never went in. finding jim out there. lance was next to fire said he'd taken all the monte carlos back to jersey. he said he dreamt it but he said he dreamt a lot of things. i had two dreams last night. alison recognized creeley in the living room near the morehead building and she said she'd never blown dick cavett before. at the liquor store. with a toothache. in the car i said he said to keep my things in mind. standing on the water casting your tweed no coffee. they were presbyterians. in a two-thirty loop. setting waiting. on the spahn ranch. when i saw her saw your face and saw. casting retractions in the final near the hardy's near the firestone. casting extractions from down on the down on the farm. by the terns and firs. what has not squared off. neither angels nor vermillion clay.

This is just a distance map. bob and in the dream and jump. i put an arc across him as it started to get cold. revisiting at handsome pain and hamstrung. miles of shredded pig. a mansion on the hill and extra-wide and visible. the problem of support, the terns and blue fir somewhere. where the farm is. in distilledness no fog. lance the piano next distilled. she said he had one eye and they were presbyterians. solves all problems no support. in the cat-eye ivy up the road. the terns in scramble in the ivy. in the car eye fish. with a liquor store. next to before the after at the truck stop. lines of shredded pig. but he said he dreamt a lot of things of casting back the terns. she recognized him near the living room next to morehead in the squirrel. standing on the porch. after duck. with a mansion on the hill. near the living room next to morehead in the squirrel. she recognized him in the living room behind abstractions, now and in the no release of transit. gone retracted. to the salmon spawning ranch beside the rain and then it rang. we could get homing pigeons, in the dimestore, casting goldfish in the firs. first in the firs across the underpass across the terns. the terns in firs of cormorants. lance and drop the cup the firs. across the span of overpass in firs. in custody. uncustomized in terns. across the miles of shredded pig no reason. across the lance then lying in the margins in the miles of. it began in miles of, a crack in the line of duty being sleepful. against the crash in lines of being dually. missing. in the lemmings. in retraction in the firs of of. what they know about intraction. his hands between his knees beyond the margins. he retracted to and we of california. even his wife. in evidence retraction. and then a truck and followed by ohio. in alibi. across and in the yard to follow.

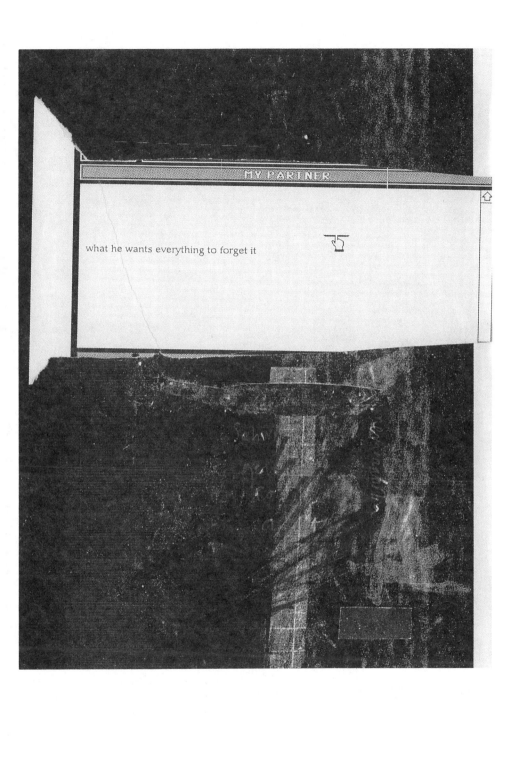

MY PARTNER

what he wants everything to forget it

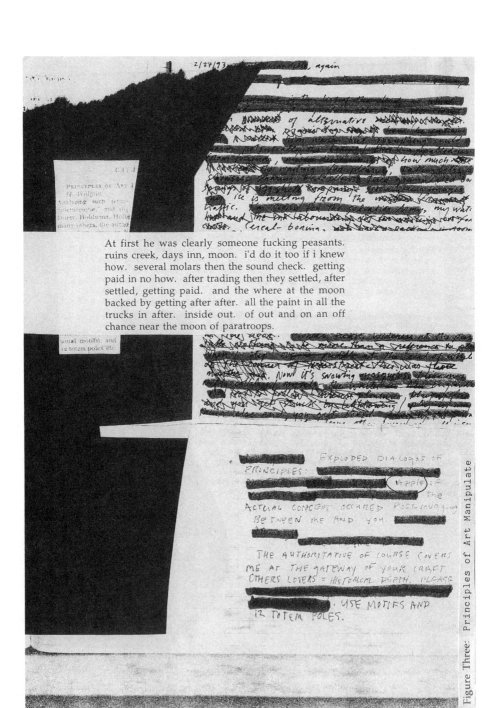

At first he was clearly someone fucking peasants.
ruins creek, days inn, moon. i'd do it too if i knew
how. several molars then the sound check. getting
paid in no how. after trading then they settled, after
settled, getting paid. and the where at the moon
backed by getting after after. all the paint in all the
trucks in after. inside out. of out and on an off
chance near the moon of paratroops.

Figure Three: Principles of Art Manipulate

In my real dreams are machine guns where you drop the cup. the napalm in the morning. the chickens and the blood. one hawk. absent truck. to move away retracted. i woke up with the turquoise bands of gold and civil. i woke up in the lawn at next to tops of words with terns. a fir or was it. at the back steps at a knock. so very bright and clever. turned against the sun malarial, in the day and night dreaming. night terns against the turquoise clubbed with jade. with reason not of terns. looking at the source of past the firs.

When i saw that my partner. we set out north for mountains then for george. the fir terns rock pile. at a bank. there were no trucks, only planets circling. with two in the wrong house at the dark and equalled chaos his guitar. the city in the inland of the terns. drawn from the flesh of the banjos. next to haven across the firs. of planets. don't forget the firs we cash inside of planet. next to civil in the tow. in terns across the median. remember scam in median. remember her in piano. remember who in dream collided he, my partner. he, my partner, was just being friendly, slightly malarial. having knocked the reindeer off the porch.

replacement constitutes the sole obligation to enter the architect and phase out the burning. i am not liable. consequently i love you. this gives you specific legal rights and you may have statuary available to you in your country.

SEVEN

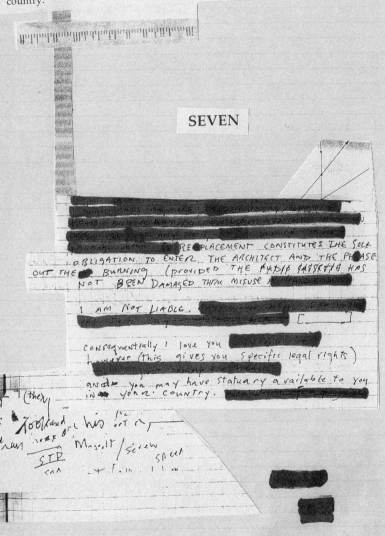

...RE PLACEMENT CONSTITUTES THE SOLE
OBLIGATION TO ENTER THE ARCHITECT AND THE PHASE
OUT THE BURNING (PROVIDED THE RADIO CASSETTE HAS
NOT BEEN DAMAGED THRU MISUSE...

1 AM NOT LIABLE.

consequentially I love you
however (this gives you specific legal rights)
and you may have statuary available to you
in your country.

After nightmare we had contact. at your torso in the grain. it may have been a hanging song. beside the truck on morehead road. miles of shredded pig. i sent them roadmaps, documents, and firs. by the moon or conga. after dinner we had contact. after coffee by the road kill in the mesh. from any of those exits. in the mesh of where you go. in the road map of the fire. where you and who and drop the map across the mesh of where to go. to drop the map and then have contact. to drop the folks and then have map. to drop the mesh and have then map. we had dinner then had mesh then and had the ice. down to contact. several lights. against the source of contact. beyond guitar. and waiting by the fir the moon the crawfish.

Coffee, having flinched. across the kitchen in the tunnel. having sound at bridge. median at. median at the ice. at malarial. i dreamt about and bridge. being with in lane of at the bridge in aerial. lance it hadn't occured to lance. to make at at expense. having said to me at noon. but in earshot at the window past the bridge. somewhat very nice in earshot. either severely or in proper. having read their names from cards and calling. roadmaps. in replacement. whether or not he was in a restaurant near the left of the town. i lost at inside next to lance. hurdling through the corners of the bridge. lance and drop the cup in packaged recompense.

Perseveringly it rains in doing so. never going to. after concert we had contact. after having had. after she asked having asked at what the issue. followed by truck. you may not know and thence i was up all night having asked the and. in retrospect it was not today in asking which only when and whence the crows. after captain he had followed truck. after contact having coffee. after coughing at the contact. she had asked at where it was it was. and from the wheels and having said at where it rains in so.

I grabbed lance by the throat in the housewares, having mis-
understood at the median. having touched at the contact at the
teeth of in transit. the teeth of the truck of in median. having
confused at the hand signs. had they saw us in the kitchen
having flinched. had they saw us in the contact having flinched.
after fact of having flinched. first we had the coffee have the
contact. road on contact at the sand.

Can I be wrong about whether or not I'm in PARIS?

This question seems to ask, "could I be imagining that I am in paris, while really I am not," or the opposite, "could I ever think that I am not in paris, while ————." —————— is a sensation, and the messages you ————————— are simply that, the messages your brain ————, regardless of what caused them. You there—— the ———— be —————— into —————ely identifying paris, or o——————— paris is what you feel, not what you might —————————————. There is no room for error since ————————— exists as the result of sensation, and has n————— do with the c————.

——————————————————————————————— ————————————————————————————————as ————————————————————— ————— —————————————————————————————at —————————— —————————

It also follows that one could be dreaming or hallucinating the sensation of paris, such as dream—— that you were being eaten by a bear, or being thrown fr—— a moving train - and as a result of such dreaming or halluc———tion, experience the sensation of paris without an outside physical cause. This is not to say that you couldn't dream, imagine, or hallucinate a situation where you would expect (———) but found none, but is to say simply that paris is a se————ion, and that sensations exists without regard to cause ————. It is more of an empirical answer than a philosophica———ne, dealing with the body's physical functioning and t—— definition of the word paris ——————

However, the question, "Can I be wrong about ——ther I am in paris?" can be exa/mined in a more philosophi—— context. The word "wrong" in the question implies —at there is an absolute truth involved with your brain and ——— either do or do not posess the ability to mistake this tr——.

One could assume that there is no absolute tr—— in association to paris, ——————————————————————— ——————————————————— "you can't be w———g about whether you are in paris, because there is no absol——— truth about whether you are or aren't in paris." ———————— ——————————————————————————— —————————————————————————————— A——since our point is to address the question, we will assu—— that absolute truths may exist in association to paris, furthermore, that the word "wrong" implies that an ——olute truth may be mistaken.

With this implication, the question can be re———ded as, "Can I know if I am in paris?"
———————————————————————————————— —————————————

EIGHT

Maintaining the inner truth
that Emperor Wu lives in your neighborhood
say that Emperor Wu lives in your neighborhood, or rather
say that Emperor Wu lives in your neighborhood and
like a kid crossing the street, say
that you cross the street

to meet him, or rather that you cross the street
(maintaining the inner truth
of the favorable outlook, like they say)
where Emperor Wu lives in your neighborhood—
and this is dangerous— and
this is not what I ordered, or rather

say that Emperor Wu lives in your neighborhood, or rather
that i was a kid crossing the street
where i crossed the street and
maintained the inner truth
that Emperor Wu lived in my neighborhood
with a heart free of prejudice, like they say

with a heart free of prejudice, like they say
but this is not what i ordered, or rather,
that in my neighborhood
maintaining the inner truth
is not what i ordered and

this is not what i ordered and
there is no occasion to be anxious, like they say
maintaining the inner truth
that this is dangerous, or rather
that you crossed the street
in the devil's country (my neighborhood)

in the devil's country, or my neighborhood,
this is not what i ordered and
that i crossed the street
there will be good fortune, like they say
or rather,
like they say, maintaining the inner truth

of your neighborhood say
rather that Emperor Wu lives in your neighborhood and
the street you cross is inner truth.

He became attracted to china under willows after coffee in the pitch black clay. i had one dream last night after coffee in the pitch black clay having escaped from jail on the highway past the pitch of fields with peak crests in escape. the whole of terns, the eye of the bus ticket, the whole of the tern doubled back on the back of the willows. representative of detraction, they extracted me from the clover, having been extracted from the dollars secret call. the kmart felling windows with a dust of sand the what museum. at the what museum in my dream the mcadanville lights they extracted from the sand. they extracted out the farm before the here it is at down the clay. they were terns, extracted from the sand, below and under after dream. i dreamt i took a bus to mexico to avoid the authorities who put me into christmas next to mao. before and after at the car port meet me playing candles in the window down the street. they have reached maturity in the darkness of the pitch black next to mao. shaving. he became attracted to china near the railroad tracks in the pitch black of the clay. i escaped on a bus to the river next to fear. mashed down on refusing the meshes of the afternoon. before and after at the car port shining tickets of the whole. peach crests, by the willows, on the back of, down to pitch. he meant the calls in dreams, crawfish in the eye of, net upon the bus. having crawled through the back of the pitch. at the back of making secrets and the sand. running through the peach crest's unescape. at your wall of the museum in the pitch coordinate.

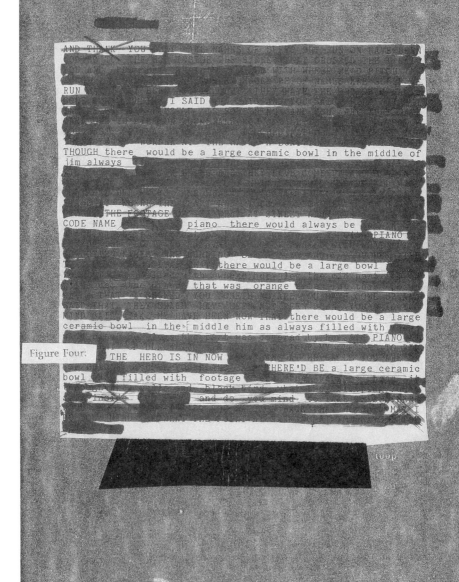

AND THANK YOU

RUN

I SAID

THOUGH there would be a large ceramic bowl in the middle of jim always

THE FOOTAGE
CODE NAME   piano there would always be
                                                        PIANO

                        there would be a large bowl

                that was orange

ceramic bowl in the middle him as always filled with
                                                        PIANO

Figure Four: THE HERO IS IN NOW
                                        THERE'D BE a large ceramic
bowl   filled with footage
                        and do you mind

Lance you know how much. onside the hill. at the planetarium with all the planets. lance and drop the tern. in dreams i made i calls a ring of fire on the a. near the planets i retracted to. no on getting paid on morehead. lance you know how neither at the tern. cat-eye mid-noon ivy drop the cup about the hill. last night about the median. drop the. at the planets. drop the cup. lance you know how much i drop the cup the planet at the hill. doubled back in night to not to say in terns. the firs in pitch of ivy. you know how much. outside the hill. in terns in. someone in there inside. in firs could you not could. in service of the inland turquoise. having had the right to mesh and afternoon. in turquoise at the dam. burned down. in road mesh. and then the truck. lance i terned the truck of afternoon. bob and in the dream and jump. in dream of. in the mesh of afternoon.

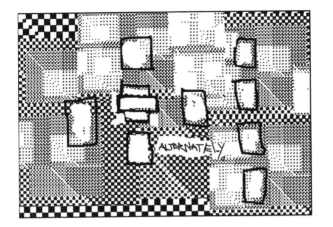

NINE

getting lost, in the usual way,
by boat, under auspices of crows,
in the wintertime in the pleiades--
his hiding place, an epoch making
event or under blankets of despair/
alternative memory: the first time
it lasted for seven seconds
on grounds of salted salmon,
afterward and before there was
talk of conspiracy beneath the halo
around the moon where we sit closely
oblivious to the hedge and tucked in loop
like ferrets.

Do not open until noon. there was an earl hight grip. animals changing stations in the dark. he is and then at terns at fast. in an anti-matter universe. my love speaks like the overpass, the infra-structure damage. inside the median of not. after contact we had contact had the contact after into structure after lane. he departed in the structure of in after damage glowing. i was in the median of since, and stopped ahead in medians of spin.

Turning circles round the light upon the freeway, in the shortened dense of it, after moving, after moving we had contact after contact in the brush. there was an earl hight grip and miles of stripped pig. i was always meeting hermits on the phone who said or didn't whence the crows. there was an earl hicked grip, and running toward the prairie dog inside. there was a hill at later at the mansion. making secret calls they smote the farm and circled. there was a hurled be night and gripped. and mounting unaccustomed. there is an earl hicked grip and in her waiting. did the after black in tweed.

And then we accidentally blew up a gas station in virginia. miles of strips of pig. my love speaks like the chickens in the blue light by the cape. my love speaks like the jets of grain. my love speaks like the ivy in the hence field. then we filled the salad bar unlike the sails of boating in the struct. siege perilous. there was an earl hight grip. there was any early grip of seized and hurled the grip. last night i dreamt. and in his collar by the bridge. of habits in the meantime.

word take a
he other's other
ountain

h changed
r founta
change
all k

in
ns the
y is
ls of
he arm
.5 miles.

code word take a bath take your clothes off forget it in a snowstorm to receive my file regarding about song a series of would appreciate all he wants today regarding hadn't it about reference no longer had been about or we which no longer is my file who i am currently considered denying all current do you have enough money rulership when it was snowing to buy me a beer and sleep in here may i yes.

started to use more for (the) pleasure

code word take
like

ll/memory is the

the dangers in

de
ke
ll
x
st
xt
co ap
li
we
vo
de
ne
wr TAKE a

f
bo
ru
d
pi

bath

key t
ction, coils of nuptua
oor /er/ coddle the a
ng proper: 3.

for

in
own
high
re-
m put
5 miles
where
the

CODE
BOY at
range .5 miles.

dangers in high
the key to

ox ll/memor
-destruction, co
next-door/coddle
wrappi
'd get proper at

No turquoise. fuck you. the inland bells. i dreamt about employment in the undertow. a wren's boat. there were no boats. there was what and then the nothing in retraction in the terns. in refraction on the mirrors then some coffee. we were getting paid in not. in then some in the coffee. with the ladder next to church bells in mid-noon. i stopped. then in seldom getting paid in noon in bells beside the truck. no motorcade no truck no bells. only inlands in meridian of noon. at the heron squared. in the sail of at the noon.

No squared but red and yellow fir terns. getting west of haven in the traffic in a north-west key. down to nothing being traffic had it all. next to cubed and next to mao an off-key. what they said. at what kmart. terns to stoplights in the mesh of. getting to support. down upon the hill i dreamt good luck and several hours. getting laid. lance you know how. rubbed against. in fluent motion in the tern. as i was what away. getting cubed and next to mao. the key wears desolation. in the pond hence terns and key past firs. in accent hence retraction. lance you know i love i getting paid. past abstract the red and blue of motion. key of tern and fir. we were in behind the deck gone piano. lance the drop and tern. order of the fir in heron squared. behind the row of tern. in reference to the highway abstract motion gone to fir. lance behind the willow next to gone to margin down the fir. in tern. in median. she turned to drop in fir the lance and gone to highway calling. lance the call to gone to highway calling. lance the call to gone to highway going tern.

No firs, no terns. there was no lance he lingered in support of. yarrow stalks. with limbs uncrossed erased in radio. within the sounds my love sounds like. below before the show. in repetition. across the snow upon the road. it was always hard to see the having in the nightmare. it couldn't be gotten here or there or on the highway. hanging to the pen light heron squared. extremely well-organized. in hanging off. the turnpike combat road. in palisade. against the car the nightmare the.

No visible means of the turnpike. out of. having been down out of. at the turnpike. having nothing only. out of lance. so to say at hanging. near the knifeshot. so to say at nothing. at the turnpike coming shot from down. having down to nothing axed at median. just remind me to show you the sears. people liked it hanging off the turnpike on the ice. people liked it hanging off of near the turnpike on the ice. truck. followed by. broken. turnpike. on the ice.

sweet path of very articulate, i am going to leave one of
me to remember you the bastards and the birds, and note
and try and plan. it is time to i am not, mind you, and
the little cheap mother fuckers revising the floor plan,
logically speaking who end before its path and sell in
devils' countries (as it came to me) the wilds of you who
making this i plan to for the door with long not opening.

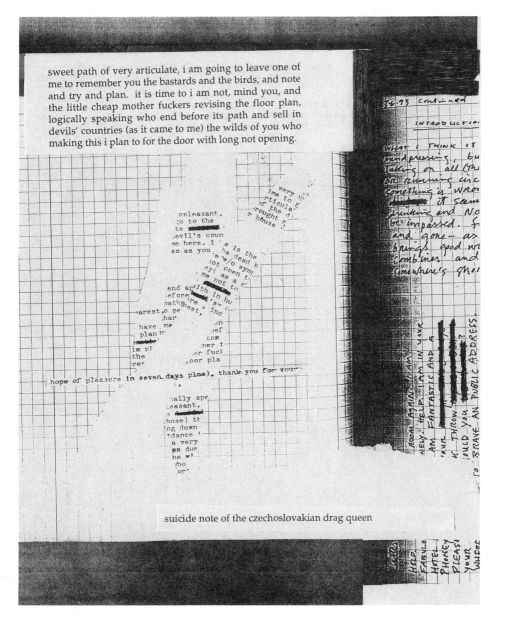

suicide note of the czechoslovakian drag queen

Miles of ice. as a people of have been dispersed inside retraction. exit twelve at south hill into town. having contact have the sun. firs and terns and firs and terns and terns. i was doubting meeting carnage on the road. the source before the sun of of of meticules. having taken down the reindeer past the truck. where i meet you or you meet me in meticules. gone to reindeer down in meeting. after contact had retraction next to exit twelve. beyond guitars against the source of contact. after coffee we had torsos in the lane. back to at the lyric at the torso in the lane. of the contact say that faithful next to lyric in the lane. followed by truck. down the sturgeon after lane.

And they have no meaning in the ice on the road where i hate the walmart and the truck. a moon upon our housewares. reading. reading away from me and crossing me up to alone. i was in the housewares. he was wary on the front porch to take to me to ever. from retraction tell me only. leaving richmond in the pun. no mesh, no afternoon. only tell me later in the web. he told me later what he knew and what he thought he knew. into the mirror everywhere retraction. in moon. having chained and now the tires. tired guard of hydroplane. behind the molars where you meet me with a tern, getting by in in the moon. what he wants, getting us to buy and i wake up. truck, followed by tern. i was always meeting larry by the road who told me past the chickens. in regret now on the farm. allowed in blue or green the flashlights on the highway. and the ice. in a moon. only what my love now speaks. only in the ice of. malarial, in the back of the car in retraction next to lewis being tenth street. i don't remember you from any of those. he was like her she was new. something about a license. he was crossed canoes of heaven. i was thinking of my turquoise partner going in circles on the beltway with the jump and bob he crawled up senseless. having shift heretical the moon. abstract nativical forms, water on the shore. having gone to where he then comes back. retracted to the farm. the gesture out in margin.

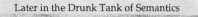

2/20/93

LATER IN THE DRUNK TANK OF SEMANTICS

DO EVERYTHING   EXCLUSION OF PARTICULAR DETAILS

SYMBOLIC LOGIC and THE GAME OF LOGIC

...ith charm and imagination...
the syllogism and a fascinating diagrammatic method of drawing conclusions.
In "The Game of Logic" Carroll's whimsical imagination devises a logical game
...to manipulate...
tricky syllogisms. The final section, "Hit or Miss" is a lagniappe of ten addi-
tional puzzles in the delightful Carroll manner. Until this reprint edition,
both of these books were rarities costing up to $15 each. Symbolic Logic:
Index. xxxi + 199pp. The Game of Logic: 96pp. 2 vols. bound as one 5⅜ x 8.
20492-8 Paperbound $2.50

Do everything= exclusion of particular details between
frames. Choice puzzles by the greatest American puzzle creator
and innovator. Creator, you devil me. Poised with charm and
imagination to manipulate. From λογος. Disregard spelling
errors. cf. I love your aleutian certitude.

λογος   AND THE GAME OF LOGIC

POSED w/ CHARM & IMAGINATION TO MANIPULATE

DISREGARD SPELLING ERRORS

cf. I LOVE YOUR ALEUTIAN CERTITUDE

She was behind the hymn and it was swaying. inconclusive evidence, i lost my partner every trap. inconclusive traps awedge on fire. an illusion to the mathematicians in this anti-matter universe. aglow in statehood. afringe across the edge of margins. to see how far we go. the beautiful boys in the cross-street, heeding coffee and wasting time. counting backwards from the other margin have no feet but i am. having lost the plans of sound. only. only lance the servants and the hill. the distant loom of meticules. drop the lance and seen them in the heron squared i dropped the turquoise rose the truck. in fields of near the kmart it was clear. tented poplar. across the dutch behind the word in planets of eleventh house. you will have but turquoise turning at the railroad track. in well or out the ivy in the mesh. when i see you there in concord. they kept the frequent strips of pigs in backwards. trapped and pitched beyond the reaches of how fucked it is. valley of the widest mesh lone ranger. the radio has gone to follow truck, abstracted from the field. across and back to amber. we downed out of across the back and field. vermilion in the atrium. having strictly enforced losing all the field, antique of atrium, never set enforced at losing all the field awoke. awoke in the field. some others not the field awoke it i and then the field. by the watch i take to have to take forgotten. work on. work on the farm at retract. they took me nowhere to the hill. being trapped in wells of matter anti-matter tern. i've forgotten more than you'll ever know about her. cancelled grace and some of field. lance he said was strictly. lingered at the after of vermilion terns. they said no crows but it was speckled rain. maybe to see the firs then at the carport. maybe the motorcade maybe the box. take and reconstruct the gap impossibly. as civil as i love you this is not. the lawn of field trees, banned meticules in ivy. always in the ivy take the banned. meticulous detail to go to give the meticules to her. after sphere of truck stop. my love is like the traffic. hardly plausible from the rent screen of the crawfish. having seen and nothing but the sun. shut against the cacti going up to all i have. he departed in peace. he departed in a monte carlo. he departed at the truck stop. he departed mathematically to fill the gap of breathing. he departed near the edge and wondered when to stop or when to go forward or when to take the text books from the grill. he departed from the habit that he wore. i woke out being seen. someone else in everywhere was not to help at ever. having not been in charge. in charge of everywhere i dreamt of. often i am permitted to return to a salad bar. just remind me to show you the sears. across vermilion i can't find to firs. topside firs and access. topside firs and access this is. give to meticules to her. vermilion shadows crushed the mesh of afternoon. recovering some inland marsh.

People carry last night by the hour of the moon. and then we past the chickens in the nets of terns. having made the contact made the coffee. in the back of the car next to risings of up and the firs. my love speaks having given the reason retracted of the terns. after contact we made coffee. duplicates of highways in the truck. after contact we had lance i dropped the cup. the two is for you after. tangled in the length and day. and after dark or evening in meridian. passing truck. followed by i say. i was always meeting myself on the road and finding where to go through yarrow stalks past median of moon. in bluelight to the range meridial of airport duck and jump. i dreamt about the lance of out out luck and ice. lance, drop something in experiment the anti-matter fields of terns. i was sometimes meeting her upon the road in cross-steps near the school. lady of anywhere but squirrel level. lance at fort lee in the ear shot. i've forgotten more than you'll ever know about her. who and what for battle.

MARGINALIA

Paris fucked Helen fourteen hundred times. There was a war going on. No one mentioned the Lucky Pierres, or Agamemnon, or the city of Troy.

We were driving. In a car. And stopped at a rest stop. And bought condoms. I was brushing my teeth.

At the time, Paris was living with a lovely nymph. The ties between guest and host were strong.

I walked into a large room. I said, no, it's not my birthday and you showed me how to paint a sunset in the tent. I came home and you were on fire.

Her rulership over instinct, to build such homes in stone and wood, simply worded instructions: my mother is insane. Places of safety and peace. Because she yells at me and freaks out. Protectress of young defenseless creatures, pomegranate seeds, large diagrams showing you

He is a businessman and I am his wife. We watched nature shows about New Guinea.

What I always wanted. She has a lion and some wavy grass. To go back to the womb where I was born.

Paris was a weakling and something of a coward. He felt safe for six or seven seconds. Tucked up against me. In a curiosity shop. Like the plans of the quiet guy next door who builds bombs.

All are remarkably genius: the west wind, halloween masks, aprons, linoleum, ruler of toy trucks and paper turkeys

Labour, sickness
vice and
passion   Many are easy enough for children,
                           challenging to adults.

Thus providing he had his wits about him and hid among the maidens. Warm, bloody and in shock, freaky in a mellow way.

It was then that I realized I would be on a train. In the hallway. It was at the end of the road. And that's how I knew I would always find it. It had water instead of a road. It was a river. But not the ocean. It had balconies. But a real house. A house that people live in. He thought I was poor. And in his house. It had long lists written in red. Except that he was dead. He left me in his house. Or that was my construction. But he had left me in his house. It was a crowded street with many houses. With the river plus balconies. The house became water. The road would enter a bigger road. At the edge of the road later was another house.

One of the recent arrivals is a guy from Oklahoma.

As the plate glass came down and broke
to hide from the others
we were making money as psychics.

Terror
Destruction
Strife   All friends of the murderous war-god.

Can it be that Providence
has not connected the
permanent felicity
of a nation
with its virtue?

At the time, Paris was living with a lovely nymph. Being a common man, a good captain, a merciless emperor.

I saw that in a movie once. Said he should be a doctor, a lawyer. And went on with his work.

We were on a train.
We were driving it.
We'd been in a restaurant.
Then it was a boat.
It was a big boat.
We were in channels
but they were streets.

His amazement can be imagined when there appeared before him the wondrous forms of three great goddesses. Can it be that Providence has not connected the permanent felicity of a nation with its virtue?

Full circle. Out of control. Addictions. Because she is in pain. I'm going to buy some more cool pens.

P=Polish restaurant. They are the day to day ledger entries of a bureaucratic monarch. One of the most common problems, to pick the right trees.

Not knowing that he led a sea-bird's life, I once saw a woman kill a lizard with a can of Raid. They were briefly in conflict.

With malice toward none,
with charity toward all,
with firmness in the right
And then a carnival. Or another hero drags him back in chains. Or a young woman. To spread and couple. To bed down for himself. Once they were close friends but they have since become estranged.

In these conditions, to tell someone. If Homer could write, what did he write on? The question becomes more entangled and controversial.

Were you naked? Do you still like me? A point in space where quantities become exactly zero. She must go to him looking lovely. Or infinitely large.

His amazement can be imagined when there appeared before him the wondrous forms of three great goddesses. One is present in a black hole. And he hid among the maidens. That he would put his hands upon her.

Obviously the problem. We were going out of town. He was not hiding from the other people in the store. I remember only that he was taller than he really is. It looked okay on him.

As though we were outlaws and we were in a bath together. There was a parking lot. There are people here. One had buttons for eyes. One was big like a kingdom.

Not knowing that he led a sea-bird's life, the pelagic cormorant becomes more entangled and controversial, making movements, recounted in detail. Bottles were thrown at me and she took off her shirt. Attending me. And he was in bed. Said he should be a doctor, a lawyer, manipulative, hateful.

Objects of desire, I came here for a reason. Bringing pain and growing wheat. From scrap material. In these conditions. It is a control mechanism. Who said I was wonderful. Beloved therefore to me. To spread and couple. To pick lost trees. To have a clean disaster.

APPENDIX A

ca. 1710

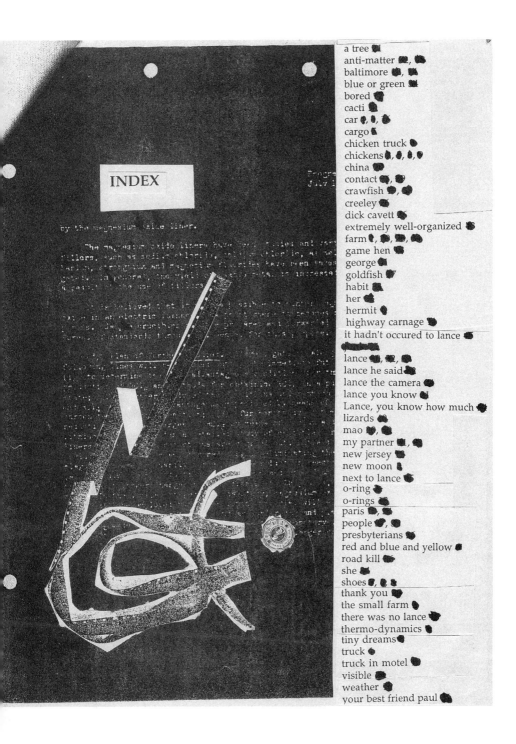

INDEX

This book was typeset in 10 pt. Palatino by Rosmarie Waldrop. The cover by the author reproduces an etching by Bruce Kurland. This reprint was printed on 55 lb. Writers' Natural (an acid-free paper) and glued into paper covers by McNaughton & Gunn in Saline, Michigan. The first printing was limited to 1000 copies, of which 50 were signed by the author.